Going Through

A Life Journey

Jackie D. Kelly

Foreword by: Jesse L. Kelly

ROYSTON
Publishing

BK Royston Publishing
P. O. Box 4321
Jeffersonville, IN 47131
502-802-5385
http://www.bkroystonpublishing.com
bkroystonpublishing@gmail.com

© Copyright – 2018

Cover Design: Kamal Designs
Cover Image by Shutterstock

ISBN-13: 978-1-946111-58-6

Printed in the United States of America

Dedication

I dedicate this book to all the men and women who have Pastored me, including my husband, who during my Christian walk implanted the seed of the Word of God in me over the years as I was learning and receiving "one day at a time." "One day at a time" was a word I heard from God in prayer once.

He said, "Take it second by second, minute by minute, hour by hour, day by day, and one day you will look back and see how far I've brought you." I learned this through the teaching I heard from these men and women of God while my husband and I were walking it out together.

Also to my children and grandchildren who gave me a will to see the future. I see God work in their lives. I am able to let my children and grandchildren see an example of not giving up and to also support and encourage them while they walk out their life journey.

Acknowledgements

This book has been a journey within itself. My precious family and church family been and continue to be a great inspiration to me, encouraging me all the way.

First, I want to thank my Lord Jesus Christ who for the last 14 years has been stretching me to make this book possible because writing a book was out of my comfort zone. This is definitely a God thing coming to pass.

I also thank my wonderful husband, Jesse. His faith in the Lord, while beside me, has helped me walk out this journey and I knew I wasn't walking alone. Jesse went through it all alongside me because we are one. When I was hurting, he was hurting too. But the Father was carrying us both. Many times, Jesse helped me in any way he could, whether it be giving me a bath, cooking something to eat, praying over and for me, or even cleaning the house. The Father truly blessed me with my great husband.

I want to gratefully thank Jackie Schoonover who choose to give me one of her kidneys when she heard a nudging from the Lord, that said, "Give her a kidney." In that selfless act I saw Jesus. Jackie has truly become a sister in my life. We may be of a different color but we are of the same spirit. I have a spiritual connection with God to pray for her and her family.

Kay Sikes, what can I say! She has worked with me effortlessly on the manuscript. Reading it! Reading it! And again, after reading it she always gave me encouragement. Thank you, Sis, for all your prayer and uplifting words to me even when I couldn't see the finished book with my eyes.

I also want to thank my sister and brothers for their prayers during those trials and attacks. All I know is that I truly love my family. So many others were there in my journey. For example, doctors and nurses who took care of me and prayed for me during the times I was in the hospitals.

My church, Pastors and saints who also had a spiritual and monetary hand in prayers for this book and in my walk of victory. And ultimately, God used Callena Fitzpatrick to direct me to Julia Royston of BK Royston Publishing. Now, I am on this journey of publishing a book and sharing it with the world. Praise God!

Table of Contents

Foreword

I am writing this in honor and at the request of my wife to express my view and account of our lives in the journey. She was inspired to write an autobiography of her life. It includes how we overcame the challenges to life through faith in God. Her desire is for me to communicate my perspective of the journey we've embarked on for the past 25 years. Her request is based on the fact that two people can experience the same event, yet the impact is different. Of course, since she is a female and I am a male, it sets us up to have dissimilar reactions and responses to similar circumstances. I will attempt to put my thoughts and reactions into words that will hopefully give the reader hope in their challenges to life and faith. All that said, let me begin by saying we were experiencing a normal life of marriage; careers, raising a family and living a faith-in-God life with all its usual problems. Our problems, we now realize, are not unique to us but are being encountered by others too. Our greatest trials of life just so happened to manifest themselves in the form of sickness of body and soul. I remember the day Jackie and I were told of her diagnosis and that she was going to need dialysis treatments three days a week. We remembered she had previously been diagnosed with lupus, but the physicians weren't sure if the renal failure was due to the effects of lupus. When we returned home from the physician's office, I curled up on the floor and we wept like babies. We didn't realize the magnitude of the life changes we faced, even though the doctor had done his best to communicate them to us. We were going to have to change our diets, daily routines, and make a huge investment in the medical expenses, which we never imagined. We recognized the test of our faith taking place in this ordeal because renal failure and dialysis is death working in the body. Many individuals just accept the facts and revolve their lives around those facts, whatever they may be. We were making the choice of acknowledging the renal failure, but we were going to revolve our lives around the truth of God. The Word of God declares that Jesus Christ bore our diseases in His body; and renal failure is a disease. So, we decided we were going to believe God's Word and walk through this valley of life by faith, Is.53:5. We realized another truth in the midst of the trials. God's unborn character (grace) is developed in our lives as we go through tribulations and tests. God's grace provides everything we need, but it is provided as we are going through this valley of death. Know this, He was bringing us through it all the time, not from it, but through it. We would not have developed the toughness of soul if we had not gone through the tribulations. We learned through all the tests that we had to make the right choices, if we were going to experience the God-desired outcomes. Every day we had to choose to follow Christ and believe what God is saying about our situation. You may feel you have no choices, but know this, you always have a choice to make. Do I believe God and His promises, or do I believe the physical evidence echoing in my mind and senses? God's taught us that His desire is that we sow to our spirit (Gal.6:7-8).

Introduction

Going Through, By: Jackie Kelly - A Life Journey *"To everything there is a season, a time for every purpose under heaven." (Eccl. 3:1)* The purpose of this book is to encourage those who have gone through, who are going through, or who will go through, trials in their lives. It is written to let you know that just because we are Christians doesn't mean trouble won't come our way. But we also need to know our Heavenly Father God will walk us through the trouble to deliver us out of it. Is. 43:2-3 says, *"When you pass through the waters, I will be with you; And through the rivers, they shall not overflow you. When you walk through the fire, you shall not be burned; nor shall the flame scorch you. For I Am the LORD your God."*

When trials come, they come to take our eyes off what God is doing in our life.

Distraction, discouragement, and defeat are the enemy's goal for us. He (Satan) wants to steal the Word planted in our heart. *John10:10- "The thief comes to steal, kill and to destroy and the Lord comes to give life and life more abundantly."*

However, when God's Word is planted in our heart, it will grow if watered, nourished, and not disturbed. That is what the enemy doesn't want to happen. He wants to get a foothold in our lives by taking the seed of the Word out of us as fast as he can--before it takes root--attacking us with everything he can find a weakness in.

I remember going through the mountains of Colorado when I saw a tree growing out of the sides of them. I believe a revelation Word came to me and said: "It took diamond blades to cut through these mountains for roads to be built because of the hard rock, but look at the trees. They found a way to grow in a hard place."

When those hard mountain places come our way, Father God wants us to find His way in order to bloom and grow. We can do one of three things: 1. Go forward 2. Stay where we are 3. Go backwards. Which one will you do? *"...that you, being rooted and grounded in love..." (Eph. 3:17)* When I started writing this book in 2003, I was **going through** many things that seemed to shake my spiritual life.

Ten years earlier, at the age of 33, I awoke one morning to tremendous pain in my body from my head to my toes. The pain was in my throat, arms, back, legs, and my ankles. The pain made it difficult to sit or walk or just to exist. The swelling in my ankles appeared like the size of a wrestler's thigh. When I took my finger and pressed on them, it left indentions, which meant that I was retaining fluid for some reason. Before I go too far, let's back up a little to see a possible root of the problem! Just before the pain in my body started, I had a spiritual battle with pain in my heart.

My mother was very ill and dying, my son had run away from home, and there was a battle in my marriage. I allowed my heart to really grieve and worry about many things. Notice that, "I allowed my heart."

There are scientific findings that say fretting and worrying can cause your immune system to weaken and expose your body to diseases. The word disease taken apart looks like (dis – ease). The Father God doesn't want us to be dis-eased but at-ease. 1 Peter 5:7 talks about *"Casting all your cares on Him (Jesus)."* Mark 4:19 says, *"The cares of this world will choke out the Word."* I believe dis-ease is what happened to me during this time. I was depressed and feeling alone, worrying about everything, had hurt feelings, and took offense about those things and others.

When I should have had **Christ Esteem,** I had Self Esteem, which was very low! I took everything said and done to me personally, and I believe that was rooted in my upbringing. This ROOT was implanted in me from generational curses that I unknowingly allowed. Says *Heb.12:15, Looking diligently lest any man fail of the grace of God; lest any root of bitterness springing up trouble..."*

Finally, I began to realize what the enemy was doing...stealing, killing, and destroying (See John 10:10). We must always find the root of the problem in order to get the victory over the problem. We must know who our enemy is, and with whom we are wrestling.

Eph.6:10-12 "Finally, my brethren, be strong in the Lord and in the power of His might. Put on the whole armor of God that ye may be able to stand against the wiles of the devil. For we wrestle not against flesh and blood, but against principalities, against powers, against the rulers of the darkness of this world, against spiritual wickedness in high places."

CHAPTER 1

"...you meant evil against me but God meant it

for good..." (Gen. 50:20)

Attack I - I was born in North Charleston, South Carolina. My family didn't have much money, so having hot running water for baths or washing dishes wasn't an option. Instead, we had to heat our water on the stove for such occasions and Attack #1 came about on one of those occasions. My sister, who was eight years old at this time, was in charge of washing dishes that day. While taking the pot of boiling water off the stove to put in the dishwashing pan, she accidentally dropped it. I was two years old and playing on the kitchen floor when the boiling water rolled under me. I received third-degree burns on my legs and hips. I don't remember much about it but my mother told me that we were too poor to spend money on hospital bills so having a skin graft was out of the question. Instead, I lay on my stomach in the hospital bed for two months. The only thing I remember about the hospital stay was looking out of the window one day and seeing a fire truck go down the street. I was on the 7th or 8th floor, so the truck looked like a small toy truck. Praise the Lord, this is the only thing I remember about this tragedy. I thank God that He knew one day I was going to marry a man who would become a firefighter. **Talk about destiny! Go Figure!**

Next Attack - After leaving the hospital, I contracted double pneumonia. My mother said the fever was so high that when I got back to the hospital, emergency room staff put me in a tub of ice water to reduce the fever. Satan had plans to kill me, but God had other plans! He was not through with me yet!

Jer. 29:11- "For I know the plans I have for you, says the Lord, plans for your welfare and not for evil, to give you a future and a hope."

CHAPTER 2

"If anyone is in Christ, he is a new creation; old things have passed away; behold, all things have become new." (1 Cor. 5:17)

 Attack II - In my youth, children teased me at school and at play. Besides being poor, my dad was not around and I had a distorted self-image of myself. I never thought I would find anyone who would want to be with me. I dated one guy in high school, but it did not work out. I was hurt and I looked at him as another man that disappointed me.   Now I know that God was setting me up for what came next.

A year later, God brought me "the man of my life" in 1973. His name was Jesse Kelly and he would become my husband. He was in the navy and we met in my hometown of Charleston. Jesse was a Christian, who grew up in a strong Christian family. While we dated, I had several encounters with Christian people telling me about the gospel. I did not really listen to them, at least not enough to change. However, I did think a lot about what they said because it scared me when they talked about going to hell. We dated while I finished high school and attended technical college in Charleston. One year later, Jesse and I had an unexpected blessing, our daughter and we named her Kesha. We moved to Texas, his hometown, where we got married. This move changed my life forever. I would never again know life as it was. In this move, I found something! This something was not just something, but Someone, and this Someone was a life charging experience! My life CHANGER was accepting Jesus Christ into my life. After accepting Christ, *there was even more.* I found a truth! It was in the Word of God! God desired that I would prosper and be in good health. ***III John 2-"Beloved, I wish above all things that*** *thou mayest prosper and be in health even as thy soul prospereth."* Years later and after being so spiritually hungry for more, I also found out that God had a gift of power for me to use. That was to be filled with the Holy Spirit. All I had to do was ask. So I asked. I received Him by faith all alone in my living room. This was when Satan really stepped up attacks on my body and tried to steal the Word from me.

The parable of the sower found in the gospels, Mark says, *"The sower (God through the Holy Spirit) sows the Word...Satan comes immediately and takes away the word that was sown in their hearts." (Mark 4:14 & 15)* Starting with the first attack at the age of two, Satan continued using "fiery darts" like bladder and kidney infections for years to set me up for what he wanted to do in my future, but the Father knew His plans for me.

As my spiritual walk got stronger, a different attack started on something else, all to distract me from my spiritual growth and to get my eyes off God. I began having trouble with my stomach; it hurt so badly. Jesse and I still believed God through every attack, holding up our shield of faith, and speaking His Word.

I remember being at a Kenneth Copeland Believer's Convention in 1979. We went to lunch at a barbeque restaurant and I believed that when I ate it, I would be fine. Instead, I began to feel pain! I was amazed that while in the midst of an awesome spiritual atmosphere with believers all around; in the midst of worship and praise; and I believed, but it would not stop! Since the attack continued, we went home and decided to go to the hospital. The examination revealed it was my gallbladder. I saw another doctor and he said I had gallstones and my gallbladder needed to come out. I had the surgery and felt so much better, but I was also disappointed. I thought I did not have enough faith to receive my healing without the surgery.

Lesson Learned Going Through: We need not be foolish in taking care of our bodies, like eating things that we know could be harmful to our body. I needed to take care of my temple, for we are the Temples of God.

I Cor. 3: 16-17 –"Know ye not that ye are the temple of God, and that the Spirit of God dwell in you? If any man defile the temple of God, him shall God destroy: for the temple of God is holy, which temple ye are."

CHAPTER 3

*"But You, O LORD, are a shield for me. My
glory and the One Who lifts up my head."
(Psalm 3:3)*

Attack III - The devil left for a season and between attacks there was always time for regrouping and resting in the Word. Then another attack came from him. From 1977-1978, I was working as an inspector for a company in Texas and began to have problems with my neck. I was required to look down through a microscope 7 hours a day, 5 days a week. When my neck began hindering me from doing my work, I decided to go have it checked out by a doctor. He said I needed to have a breast reduction to relieve the weight on my shoulders. So I did. However, come to find out it, wasn't my breasts after all. Instead, it was the position at my job that was causing the pain because when I returned to the job, the pain resumed.

Jesse and I decided it was best to let the job go and the pain stopped. I allowed myself to be stolen from again, but God was still with me through all my failures and teaching me all the way. **Lesson Learned Going Through: When I fall, He picks me back up. No Camping Out! But Going Through! Shaking It OFF! Trying Again!** Soon after this, we started planning for a baby. We were very happy to have a boy because we really wanted a son. As a matter of fact, while I was pregnant with him and before sonograms existed to tell you the sex of the child, I received a Word from the Lord saying I was going to have a son. So I only bought boy's clothing and considered only boy's names. Some people thought that we were looney, but we didn't care. Jesse told some people at work we were going to have a boy and they laughed at him. He said the

Lord spoke to him through the Word, and told me *"don't cast your pearls before swine because they will trample them." (Matt.7:6)* When it was time, it was a boy! We could have said, "See, I told you so," but we didn't. After Keanon was born, the enemy tried to attack him. The doctor wanted us to put him in the hospital to do some test because they thought they saw something unusual during an examination. We did as suggested while praying every step of the way with the saints. They couldn't find a thing after three days of hospitalization. Finally, Jesse looked at me and said, "That's it! Pack everything! We are going home and call for the elders and lay hands on him and he will be just fine." (James 5:14) And Keanon was just fine. Some months after his hospital stay, the enemy began to attack our baby boy again. It seemed that for a few years around Thanksgiving and Christmas, our son was attacked. The prayer chain came out again and I would pray, "God, this is the Son you gave us, the devil can't have him." Finally, Keanon's tonsils were removed and he was fine. Four months after my son's tonsils were removed, I got pregnant with my last son, which was unexpected but such a blessing to have two sons and a daughter now. We believed God to give us one boy and got two!

CHAPTER 4

*"My sheep hear My voice, and I know them,
and they follow Me." (John 10:27)*

 Attack IV A few years after my last son, Kevin, was born I began to have problems with my joints. I felt like an elderly woman. When I sat down and got up, every joint I had hurt so badly. Jesse and I prayed faithfully and we took it to the elders and saints to pray also. We were "going through" but not setting up camp. Finally, I went to my doctor and he did several lab tests. After finding the results, he sent me to a kidney specialist. He wanted me to do a 24-hour urine test, which was very embarrassing to me. I know this was pride, but I had to bring urine in a BIG orange jug, though the hospital halls, with everyone looking at me (so I thought)! But, I did it anyway. A week passed when I got the news. The news I received from him was not good. He said the test showed I had too much protein in my urine and it was not good for my body. Too much protein in your body can shut down a person's kidney and many other organs. So I decided to take treatment for the disease (dis–ease) called proteinosis. The treatment was a steroid called prednisone, and it did help, but it also reacted with my body very badly. I blew up like a balloon and my blood pressure escalated. Along with other problems, I went from a size 12 to 18, which was depressing in itself. At times, I felt like I didn't want to go on.

Then one Saturday, I went to a women's program at church. The program was great. However, the thing that really spoke to me was when I entered the restroom. Yes, the restroom is where I saw the writing on the wall! There on the wallpaper was written a message from God to me...the words "NEVER, NEVER, EVER, GIVE UP!!" This statement was another life-changer for me! I started getting into the Word of God more and more, taking it more and more personally. I would read, _**Is.53:5 – "He was wounded for my transgressions and bruise for my iniquity with His stripes I am healed**._" I would pray healing scriptures every day and believing the Lord for my healing. I would also do all that I knew to do and just stand, just like the Word says to do. _**(Eph. 6:13 – "...and having done all, to stand.")**_

Out of this attack, God give me a song that I recorded called, I'll Trust You Lord . These are the verses I was given. Verse 1: Trials and Tribulations that I've gone through you've always been there to see me through. Arm stretch out wide to wrap around me, just like a father should all ways do. That's why, I'll Trust you Lord –repeat 3 times.

The 2nd verse: The power of Your Word has brought me through, in those time I didn't know what do, in your word I've found life and peace, just where said I need to be. That's why, I'll trust You Lord. Repeat this 3 times.

CHAPTER 5

"I beseech you therefore, brethren, by the mercies of God, that you present your bodies a living sacrifice, holy, acceptable to God, which is your reasonable service."
(Romans 12:1)

 Attack V Well, I began to get better. I was walking 3 miles a day and lost 30 pounds. It was around 1999, three years had passed, and I became a little slothful in the Word again.

In February of 2000, after my brother committed suicide, I began to feel those old feeling again. **I WAS HURTING,** from my head to my toes again. I said to myself, **Oh No! Not again!** So, I went in to see the doctor and again he sent me to a specialist. The specialist wanted me to have a muscle biopsy. Well, I did and it came back positive for inflammation of the muscles, which they called myelitis. The doctor said I needed a medicine called Cytosine, which is a form of chemotherapy. So in September 2000, I started chemo. When I started the treatment, I had a little fear that tried to creep in, but the Lord said not to be afraid. This meant I had many changes I needed to make in my life. I could no longer put any chemical in my hair, and I had to drink canned milk supplements. The hair on my head began to shed when I combed it, and I just cried thinking that I might lose all my hair, but praise God I didn't. As a matter of fact, I didn't even get sick and threw up anytime but just an unsettled stomach, THANK GOD!

CHAPTER 6

"My brethren, count it all joy when you fall in various trials knowing that the testing of your faith produces patience." (James 1:2-3)

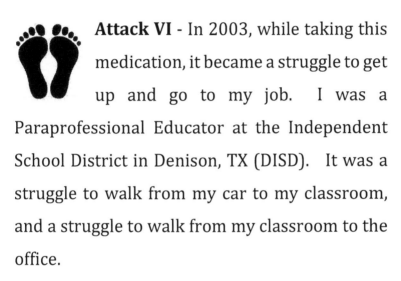 **Attack VI** - In 2003, while taking this medication, it became a struggle to get up and go to my job. I was a Paraprofessional Educator at the Independent School District in Denison, TX (DISD). It was a struggle to walk from my car to my classroom, and a struggle to walk from my classroom to the office.

I found myself having problems breathing. I asked myself, "Why am I having problems breathing?" I called the doctor to ask why. I made an appointment to see him, went in, and got some news that I didn't want to hear. Well, here we go again! I was still on 60 mg of prednisone. The medicine caused me to retain fluid that I could not get rid of, my blood pressure would not come down, and I was wheezing when I breathed.

My doctor said to me, "I want to put you in the hospital."

I said no! He agreed to try to get the blood pressure down with some stronger medicine, but if that didn't work, he was sending me to the hospital. Unfortunately the meds didn't work, so I was in the hospital for a few days. This ordeal began the days of testing of my faith, but the Lord told me not to be afraid and to trust Him because this too would pass.

2 Cor. 4:17 says, "For our light affliction, which is but for a moment."

Then, all the saints began to pray again! I could feel the prayer of the saints. I felt the peace of the Lord all over me. The nurses would come in and say to me that I looked so calm. I would say to them that it was just the peace of the Lord from the prayer of the saints. While in the hospital, the doctor had more tests performed on me and they didn't show good news. One of the tests performed was a kidney biopsy, and the results were not what I wanted to hear. I was told my kidney was not getting rid of the fluid from my body and that was why I had gained so much weight. The doctor said that I was wheezing because I had fluid around my heart and lungs. Then he said that they were going to start Dialysis. This meant, I needed to have two surgeries. One surgery to place a central venous catheter in my neck and the other to create a vein in my arm, called an arteriovenous fistula (AV). The AV was to be permanent and allowed for the dialysis treatments that occurred every other day, 3 days a week for 3-4 hours per treatment. I felt like Job in the Bible. Job 1:1-20 tells the story of a man that lost everything and God restored everything back to him in the end.

CHAPTER 7

"Who Himself bore our sins in His own body...by whose stripes you were healed." (I Pet. 2.24)

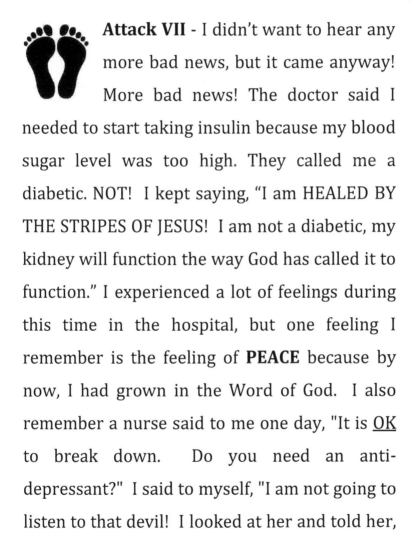 **Attack VII** - I didn't want to hear any more bad news, but it came anyway! More bad news! The doctor said I needed to start taking insulin because my blood sugar level was too high. They called me a diabetic. NOT! I kept saying, "I am HEALED BY THE STRIPES OF JESUS! I am not a diabetic, my kidney will function the way God has called it to function." I experienced a lot of feelings during this time in the hospital, but one feeling I remember is the feeling of **PEACE** because by now, I had grown in the Word of God. I also remember a nurse said to me one day, "It is <u>OK</u> to break down. Do you need an anti-depressant?" I said to myself, "I am not going to listen to that devil! I looked at her and told her,

"NO! I don't need anything! I can feel the prayer of the saints, I feeling Gods peace." She looked amazed that I was saying this because she knew what the doctors were saying about me. (Later, I found out that nurse was amazed about the glory of the Lord on me at that time. I kept a smile on my face and was not being move by what was going or what I was hearing. *II Cor.4:18-While we look not at the things which are seen, but at the things which are not seen: for the things which are seen are temporal, but the things which are not seen are eternal.)* Whose report was I going to believe? **When did Jesus heal me?** Was it the day I asked him, or was it the day that He received the STRIPES on His back and died for me? Yes, it was the day that He received the stripes and died and took the keys back from the devil, and rose again. NOW, all my body had to do was to receive my healing. The scripture says, *"Now! Faith is the substance of things*

hoped for and evidence of things not seem."
(Heb. 11:1) The day I left the hospital to come home, was a very trying day. The changes I had to make were overwhelming. My husband and I walked through the front door and sat down. Just then, it seemed like everything that had happened hit us like a brick in the face. We laid on each other's shoulder and just cried. Then we looked at each other and said, "We will make it through!" We reminded each other of Isaiah 43:2-3, which says, *"When you pass through the waters, I will be with you; And through the rivers, they shall not overflow you. When you walk through the fire, you shall not be burned, Nor shall the flame scorch you. For I am the Lord your God, the Holy One of Israel, your Savior..."* We knew we were Going Through! We were not setting up camp here! We were not pitching a tent in this mess and repeatedly

saying woe is me, for God was with us to help us
through.

CHAPTER 8

"My son, attend to my words; incline thine ear unto my sayings. Let them not depart from thine eyes...for they are life unto those that find them, and health to all their flesh." (Prov. 4:20-22)

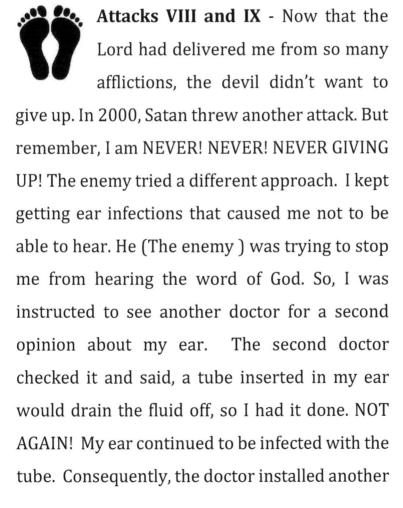 **Attacks VIII and IX** - Now that the Lord had delivered me from so many afflictions, the devil didn't want to give up. In 2000, Satan threw another attack. But remember, I am NEVER! NEVER! NEVER GIVING UP! The enemy tried a different approach. I kept getting ear infections that caused me not to be able to hear. He (The enemy) was trying to stop me from hearing the word of God. So, I was instructed to see another doctor for a second opinion about my ear. The second doctor checked it and said, a tube inserted in my ear would drain the fluid off, so I had it done. NOT AGAIN! My ear continued to be infected with the tube. Consequently, the doctor installed another

tube, and one after another one, and another one, and another one and another one. Finally, I said enough already! No more tubes, Lord! I give up; show me what I need to do. So, He did!

Trust Me on this! No more tubes! So I trusted God! Well, I got my ear settled, and then the enemy attacked my eyes to keep me from seeing God's Word. I had a problem focusing on things close up. One doctor said my eye problem was from old age, and another said that it was glaucoma and that I needed drops in my eyes.

Here's another opportunity for the Lord to show Himself strong in me. I stood on His Word, believing that I would be delivered from medicine drops. The doctor said that he wanted to do surgery on my eyes. But I wasn't sure I want to, but I did. So, after he did the right eye he said that he would do the left eye later. A year later when I went in for an eye checked, he asked was I still using the drops in my eyes, I said sometime but not often. When they checked my eyes, the pressures in both eyes, they had became normal. No more drops to this day...Glory be to God!

Lesson Learned Going Through: The Father uses us as a lightning rod to show His power when we stand and expect all that He has for us.

CHAPTER 9

*"Set your affection on thigs above, not on
things on the earth." (Col. 3:2)*

 Attacks X Another attack came in the
form of spots (loss of pigment) on my
back, arms, ear, and face. I went to the
doctor to see what was going on in the flesh, for
I know what was going in the spiritual realm.
The doctor called it Vitiligo, another something
that dealt with my immune system, so I needed
to get ready for battle again. This attack may
seem like nothing to some people, but for me, I
received the news hard. Why? I used to have a
low self-esteem and in certain situations,
sometimes it tries to creep back in. This attack
was one of those situations. I started
entertaining the thought of looking like a spotted
ugly person, and mostly on my face! This thought
made me feel depressed, but I came to my senses

and realized what was going on and who was doing this.

I said to myself, "Jackie, don't go there, for that's not a good place to go." Then, I called on the saints to agree with me for healing. After a few months, I was looking in the mirror and noticed that the spots on my face and ear were gone. Thank God! He gets the glory!

Lesson Learned Going Through: When we start going to "those places not of God" it is not a good thing to think about. For example, when you see something really filthy and dirty, if you are like me, you don't want to touch it. If a restaurant is dirty, I feel very hesitant about eating there. Consequently, when my husband says, let's go to so and so restaurant and I know it is not clean, I usually say, "Let's not go there." That's what we should say when we hear thoughts, or see things coming up in our lives that are not of God.

Phil. 4:8 says, *"Finally, brethren, whatsoever things are true, whatsoever things are honest, whatsoever things are just, whatsoever things are pure, whatsoever things are lovely, whatsoever things are of good report; if there be any virtue, and if there be any praise, think on these things."* **Therefore,** let's learn to do this for everything that doesn't appear to be something God would have for us to do.

CHAPTER 10

"Then beware lest thou forget the Lord, which brought thee forth out of the land of Egypt, from the house of bondage." (Deut. 6:12)

Attacks XI In 2003, the Lord delivered me from dialysis treatments in six months. Three months later, I was healed from diabetes. During the five years after being set free from the dialysis machine, I began to see subtle attacks from the enemy, but ignored them. Instead, I found myself getting very comfortable in my past victories, which is still another trap of the devil. I was going through a "mountain" time. This is when you feel like everything is going well and you are on the top of everything. I became **BUSY** (**B**uried **U**nder **S**atan's **Y**olk) doing things that were good, but that caused me to neglect the Father's business and slacked off reading and speaking the Word and praying. I just didn't do what God was telling me to do, which was forgetting where He brought me from and being thankful and giving God the glory daily. Consequently, I gave the enemy a foothold to come in again. I found myself at that place when my lab levels began to decline again. My doctor told me I needed to have another kidney biopsy. I was disappointed with this news. Then I began to feel like I had let God and myself down for not eating right, exercising, and quoting the Word like I should.

Then I heard the Lord say to me, "Am I not bigger than what you can do?" He said, "If exercising, eating, and just quoting my Word was all it took, then you could get the glory. The Glory is not yours, it's Mine!" He reminded me of the scripture, John 9:1-3 that says, *"And as Jesus passed by, he saw a man which was blind from his birth. And his disciples asked him saying, Master, who did sin, this man, or his parents, that he was born blind? Jesus answered, Neither hath this man sinned, nor his parents: but that the works of God should be made manifest in him."* (In other words, THAT GOD BE GLORIFIED).

Lesson Learned Going Through: Never take the glory for what God has done. So now, what I say is: "For God's glory I have a new kidney, For God's glory that Lupus no longer lives in my body, or for God's glory my whole body is healed by the stripes of Jesus." **It is for God's glory that Jesus did what He did for you and me.**

CHAPTER 11

"Now unto him that is able to do exceeding abundantly above all that we ask or think, according to the power that worketh in us." (Eph. 3:20)

 Attacks XII   In 2008, there was another attack to my kidney and I was back on dialysis for the second time. Throughout the attack I believed, this is not for long! I had no idea how and when I would be off, all I knew was, I will be!   As I went week after week to the dialysis center, I continued to do as I told. One day the doctor asked, "Do you want to get a kidney transplant?" I really wanted to hear from the Lord about this, so I said that I would think about it.

One night I asked the Lord, "How are you going to heal me this time?" Because there weren't any apparent donors, my sister volunteered but they wouldn't accept her kidney and other family members were not able. It just seemed like I couldn't hear an answer.

Two years later, I was speaking at a care group about my testimony. I spoke about how God delivered me from dialysis the first time, and how I believed God would get me off dialysis again. Unknown to me, God was speaking to someone at the group about giving me a kidney. The weekend after the group, a sister named Jackie Schoonover came to me and said, "If you decide to have a kidney transplant, I believe God wants me to give you one of mine."

At the time, I was not sure what the Lord wanted to do. But I was thinking to myself, "This isn't a nickel, I can't give it back." It's an organ, that can't be returned." I told her I would let her know. One thing I knew for sure if I decided to do the transplant, I wanted a live donor because it is a better kidney for a transplant.

Weeks passed, but while waiting to hear from God, I heard a testimony from someone about a man and his wife. They said the husband was waiting on a kidney for transplant but wasn't finding a match. Then his wife asked him to let her try to see if she was a match for him. At first, he didn't want her to because he didn't want both of them to be down from surgery. Finally, he finally agreed to let her try. She was a perfect match! The greatest part was when they went in for her kidney, the doctors found that she had three!

She told her husband, "See, God had your new kidney in me all along!"

When I heard this story, I believed God said to me, "Don't put Me in a box. I can use whatever or whoever I choose to heal you."

This was when I told Jackie, "Let's do it!" I told Jackie what she needed to do and she did. We found out she was a match for me, but it took three years from that time until the scheduled transplant. In the interim, the enemy tried to kill me three times. Once, I was on life support for two days, and two other machines before life support. During this journey, my husband, family, and church family supported me. I never lost hope of being delivered from all of this. I was tired, but not faithless.

Jesse would say, *"Jesus is praying for us that our faith fails not because Satan desires to sift you like wheat."* (Luke 22:31 -32)   As I walked on this journey, God used the story of Joseph to encourage me. I saw people being blessed who came in my presence. They would tell me that my life of being faithful had really blessed them. God was using what the enemy meant for my bad, to turn it for my good. (Genesis 50:20). My testimony has not been in vain, but for the glory of God. (Gen. 39:5) says,

"... the Lord blessed the Egyptian's house for Joseph's sake...."

CHAPTER 12

"It shall come to pass in the last days, saith God, I will pour out my Spirit upon all flesh; and your sons and your daughters shall prophesy, and your young men shall see visions, and your old men shall dream dreams." (Acts 2:17)

 The blessing of a new kidney from Jackie came on December 4, 2012. We checked in the hospital for surgery early that morning. Our family members and pastors came to show support and to pray in faith and agreement with us. While we were waiting in our separate rooms to prepare for the surgery, my nurse came in and introduced herself to us, saying "My name is Jackie. I will be taking care of you today." We all looked at each other, and said, "Another Jackie? Three Jackies!" I felt like the Lord was giving me a confirmation that everything was going to be just fine.

The number three signifies the Father, Son, and Holy Spirit. They were all with me. We both were covered by the Triumphant Threesome. The transplant took longer than expected, but it was successful. The doctors said that soon after they hooked up Jackie's kidney to my body it began to make urine. They told Jesse the first 24 hours were crucial so they watched me very closely to make sure all was going well.

Within 24 hours, I was told that my labs were off causing the doctors to have concerns. It seems like when I am in these conditions I can always feel the prayers of the saints. Jesse, who hardly ever remembers any of his dreams, came to me the next morning and told me of a dream or vision he had. He said that he saw himself in a field covered with deep green grass, almost black in color and about knee high. In this grass were little rat-like creatures that he couldn't see until they would jump up and nip him on the hands.

He said when he would hit at them they ran away. Off in the distance was a large figure that looked like Star Wars character Darth Vader. He started to talk to this figure of a man and said, "What is that?" The figure said, "My pet! You just leave it alone!" At that time he awoke and asked the Lord, "What was that all about?" The Lord told him, "The enemy is trying to steal your wife's new kidney so you go take authority over him and stop it." That was when I remember Jesse coming up to my room, telling me about it, and laying hands on me to pray. When the next labs or two came, the report was good. I am very grateful for Jackie's gift of her kidney. It truly was a sacrifice because she can't get it back. We are truly spiritual sisters. Sometimes I can sense when I need to pray for her, which I try to do when it happens. This is just my side of the story about the transplant, but I believe that Jackie Schoonover's side is very important too because she heard from the Lord to give the kidney and upon hearing, she obeyed. God is so great and His mercy endures forever!

CHAPTER 13

"...I will never leave thee, nor forsake thee."
(Heb. 13:5)

 Attack XIII In 2014, we were still rejoicing over my new kidney given to me by a work from God when the enemy comes in like a flood again, to steal, to kill, and to destroy. This time his modus apparatus was a car accident. Jesse was driving and I was asleep so my body didn't take the impact of the crash as hard as it would have been if I was awake and bracing myself. I also know God had His angels around us because we both could have had worst injuries than we had. Praise God! An ambulance took me to the nearest hospital to be checked out for injuries because I was experiencing pain in my lower and mid sections. Before the ambulance left, Jesse called our daughter, Kesha, to pick him up since our car was wrecked. Faith had it that she worked for an insurance company Praise the Lord, for showing us favor! Kesha was also able to give her Dad directions on where to get a rental car. After contacting our insurance company and checking three rental places, Jesse had a rental car in three hours. This was very important because our home was an hour away. While waiting on x-rays at the hospital, we didn't consider anything serious was wrong, but after I passed out in the restroom, the doctors put a rush on my tests. They discovered I was bleeding internally and needed a transfer to another hospital that handled trauma. When I arrived, I was taken to trauma #3. GOD WAS DOING THINGS IN threes and I felt like He was giving us a "God Wink" and just letting us know He was carrying us through this attack too as He said in Isaiah 43:2-3. The trauma team had to remove 10 inches of my small intestine that was damaged. The doctors said my healing would come quickly so I was released after 7 or 8 days. After getting home and settling down for bed, Jesse received a "wake-up call" from the Lord at 4:00 in the morning. He felt like the Lord was saying to him, "Go to the hospital!" He listened and obeyed. When Jesse got to the Emergency Room, there were no other patients waiting so they took him right in. They took x-rays, which showed that all this time he had two broken ribs, but God sustained him through the pain during my recovery! Praise God!!

CHAPTER 14

"I am crucified with Christ: nevertheless I live; yet not I, but Christ liveth in me: and the life which I now live in the flesh I live by the faith of the Son of God, who loved me, and gave himself for me." (Gal. 2:20).

The Life I Now Live There were some moments in my journey when I felt very weak in my mind, body, and spirit, but God gave me these Words about Moses. He reminded me of when Moses was standing on the hill with the rod (which for me now is the Word of God) fighting the battle. When Moses' arm would get tired and the rod began to come down, they would begin to lose the battle, so Aaron and Hur came **alongside** and helped hold up the rod! That's what I needed. The Lord said to me let the saints come alongside and help you hold up the stick of faith until the battle is won. **And they did!** Many people in my life were praying and giving me encouragement.

The enemy came to kill me, but the Lord spoke to me through Psalm 118:17, that says, *"I shall not die, but live, and declare the works of the Lord."*

The Bible also says, *"The thief cometh not, but to steal, and to kill, and to destroy..." (John 10:10).* So any attacks on me would not stand because God was on my side to deliver me out of them. Praise God! I know going through those things was a test. Believing that God is with me: The Lord said we will **go through** trials in our life but He will be with us. *"When you pass through the waters, I will be with thee; and through the rivers, they shall not overflow thee; when thou walk through the fire, thou shalt not be burned; neither shall the flame kindle upon thee."* **(Is. 43:2)**

For we know that trials come only to make us strong. Rom.5:2-3, 6 says, *"By whom also we have access by faith into this grace wherein we stand, and rejoice in hope of the glory of God. And not only so, but we glory in tribulation also: knowing that tribulation worketh patience; For when we were yet without strength, in due time Christ died for the ungodly."*

And in James, *"My Brethren, count it all joy when ye fall into divers temptations; Knowing this, that the trying of your faith worketh patience." (James 1:2-3)*

Paul said in II Cor.4:8-10 that, *"We are troubled on every side yet not distressed: we are perplexed, but not in despair; Persecuted, but not forsaken; cast down, but not destroyed; Always bearing about in the body the dying of the Lord Jesus, that the life also of Jesus might be made manifest in our body.*

Though troubles confront us in our lives, Jesus says that He would be manifested in us. But we must allow Him to, by believing and trusting in Him and the words of the Father.

And again in vs. 17-18, *"For our light affliction, which is but a moment, worketh for us a far more exceeding and eternal weight of glory. While we look not at the things which are seen, but at the things which are not seen: for the things which are seen are temporal; but the things which are not seen are eternal."* He said our light afflictions are just for a moment and it works a more *exceeding* and *eternal* weight of glory. Webster says that *exceeding* means extraordinary, extreme, or surpassing. The word *eternal* means existing through all time; forever the same; always true or valid; and unchanging seeming never to stop. The word *Glory* is worshipful adoration or praise, the condition of high achievement. The Father is saying for us not to focus on the things we see happening in our life because it temporary, but the things we don't see, which are spiritual, are eternal. This may sound backward, but our Father is pleased by our faith.

"But without faith it is impossible to please him: for he that cometh to God must believe that he is and that he is a rewarder of them that diligently seek him." (Heb. 11:6)

The Lord wants us to hold on to our profession of our faith: *Heb.10:23- "Let us hold fast the profession of our faith without wavering; (for he is faithful that promised)".* That is what the enemy wants us to do, which is to let go of our confession. He knows the power of our words. If he can get us to say what he said and not what God said then he has won the victory over us. That's why Satan attacks our thought life. This is just one of the weapons he uses, negative_ ***thinking.*** _This weapon is designed to steal the Word of God that has been sown in you and me. *Proverb 23:7- For as he thinketh in his heart, so is he:*

Proverb 4:23- Keep thy heart with all diligence; for out of it are the issues of life.

Right now, making sure I am guarding my heart against the enemy is the most important thing to me.

CHAPTER 15

"He has put a new song in my mouth; Praise to our God. Many will see it and fear and will trust in the Lord." (Ps. 40:3).

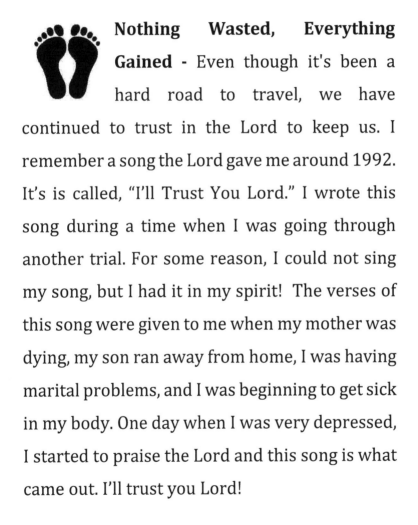 **Nothing Wasted, Everything Gained** - Even though it's been a hard road to travel, we have continued to trust in the Lord to keep us. I remember a song the Lord gave me around 1992. It's is called, "I'll Trust You Lord." I wrote this song during a time when I was going through another trial. For some reason, I could not sing my song, but I had it in my spirit! The verses of this song were given to me when my mother was dying, my son ran away from home, I was having marital problems, and I was beginning to get sick in my body. One day when I was very depressed, I started to praise the Lord and this song is what came out. I'll trust you Lord!

The first verse is, **[Trials and tribulations that I've gone through; You've always been there to see me through. Arms stretched out wide to wrap around me just like a father should always do.]**

The second verse says: **[The power of Your Word has brought me through in those times that I didn't know what to do. In Your Word I've found life and peace, just where You said I need to be.]** The second verse was not given to me until six years after the first verse.

At that time I said, "I hope one day to publish this song so others can be blessed by the song like I am blessed." I did have it recorded and I was able to share it with many others who were blessed to hear it.

II Chron.16:9 –says: For the eyes of the Lord run to and fro throughout the whole earth, to show himself strong in the behalf of them whose heart is perfect toward Him. Father wants us to know that He is watching over us, to show Himself strong if we are focused on Him to trust Him.

Victory Report - For Gods glory! I can now say, that lupus is no longer active in my body. I received a lab report in October 2007 confirming that lupus was negative and there was no sign of it.

Here Are Some Other Lessons I've Learned In The Times Of Going Through

Seeking God's Ways, Path & Will Foundational scripture: Proverb 3: 5 - <u>Trust</u> in the Lord with all thine heart: and <u>lean not</u> unto thine own understanding: In all thy ways acknowledge him and he shall direct thy <u>path.</u>

 Seeking - Means to try to find, look for, ask for, aim at, or find out by asking and searching

Trust - A firm belief or confidence in honesty, integrity, reliability, justice, of another person or thing: faith; reliance

Ways - Methods, position, manner

Path - A manner or course of conduct, thoughts, or procedure

Lean - Your assessment of or your intelligence of

We are in a fight, but the battle is not ours but the Lord's (2 Chronicles 20:15).

The writer said in Psalm 119:11, "Thy Word have I laid up in my heart, that I might not sin against thee." I consider God's Word as jewels. A "jewel" is a precious stone, a gem, a person, or thing of great value and rare excellence. That's why it is so important to share it whenever we can. It is seed to the sower.

Luke 17:5-9 starts with the Apostles. In verse five, the apostles ask Jesus to increase their faith. Out of that request came these statements from Jesus. Verses 6 -10: Verse 6: And the Lord said, if ye had faith as a grain of mustard seed, ye might say unto this sycamine tree, be thou plucked up by the root, and be thou planted in the sea; and it should obey you. Vs. 7 – But which of you [A Master], having a servant plowing or feeding cattle, will say unto him by and by, when he is come from the field, Go and sit down to meat [eat]? Vs. 8- And will not rather say unto him, Make ready wherewith I may sup, and gird thyself [Put on an apron], and serve me, 'til I have eaten and drunken, and afterward thou shalt eat and drink? Vs.9- Doth he thank that servant because he did the things that were commanded him? I trow not. [Of Course Not]. In the same way, when we are working our faith, which is a seed, it obeys. It is doing what it is supposed to do. Faith will work if we work our faith! It is obeying to bring forth a harvest. When the Apostles asked Jesus to increase their faith, His reply in verse 6 was to get them to see they had that faith, they just needed to use it by speaking to the situation. It isn't the size of the mustard seed, it was what you do with the seed. You plant the seed by what you are saying. Words are the seeds to plant our faith.

We must put it in good ground. Mark 4:8 ...Fell on good ground, and did yield fruit that sprang up and increased... The harvest will come, but we must feed the servant of faith. (Faith must be fed). Luke 17:8. How do we feed our faith? Roman 10:17 - "So then faith comes by hearing and hearing from the Word of God." The Bible has many examples of word of faith people: The book of Hebrews 11 has examples of old testament saints like: Abraham, Joseph, Moses, Rahab and many more. All these were before-the-cross faith believers. So being on this side of the cross (GRACE) how much more shall we believe.   Seed is the way the Kingdom works. Genesis 10:22- While the earth remaineth, there will be seedtime and harvest....Mark 4:26-So the Kingdom of God is as if a man should cast unto the ground; 27- And should sleep, and rise night and day, and the seed should spring up and grow up, he knows not now.   The kingdom walk works! Let us keep it before us on our journey. This walk will bring us through our "Going Through" for we are not alone. My life has been a daily walk by faith. II Corinthians 5:7, "For we walk by faith, not by sight." John 14:26 says, "He will bring to your remembrance all things that He said to you." It is truly the Word of God that we need to remember.

Things to Remember

The list of <u>Things to Remember</u> will help you and me when walking through life as it happens.

 Do not **murmur and complain:** *Hinders your prayers. Phil. 2:14, Ps. 77:3, Ex.14:8*

Do not to take offense. Ps. 119:65

Do not to lose your peace. Phil 4:6-7, Col. 3:15 Stay Focused.

Keep your eyes on Jesus and His finished work. For what you focus on, is what you get, like taking a picture. The image is what you are focusing on.

Don't focus on the bad, because; *Hebrew 11:1-Now faith is the substance of things hope for the evidence go things not seen.*

Put on the garment of praise. *Is. 1:3, Ps. 149:1 Ps. 51:15*

Stay committed to the word. Ps. 31:1, Ps. 37:5. *Have an attitude of change.* Rom. 12:2, Phil. 4:2 **LEARN how to CAST DOWN (*THROW DOWN) IMAGINATIONS.*** I Cor. 10:5

The Battle is not <u>YOURS.</u> It's the Lord's! II Chron. 20:15-16.

When you have done all to STAND, STAND THEREFORE. EPH.6:14.

WATCH what you say. Speak the Word. Proverb 4:24, 6:2, 10:11 ,13:2-3

Keep a MERRY HEART. It does good like medicine. Proverb 15:13, 17:22

Get rid of PRIDE. DON'T EVEN LET IT IN! Proverb 16:18-20.

SEEK THE KINGDOM OF HEAVEN FIRST. For it is: Righteousness, peace, joy in the HOLY GHOST. Rom.14: 7. Matt 6:33- Seek first the Kingdom and His righteousness and all these things shall be added unto you.

Do not let Satan steal your joy. Rom. 5:11,
I Peter 1:8, I john 1:4. Neh. 8:10 - ....The Joy of the
Lord is our Strength.

Guard your HEART. *Proverb 23:19.*
Proverb - Keep your heart with all diligence for
our top it are the issues of life.

Look unto Jesus the author the finisher
of our faith. *Hebrews 12:2.*

Let not your heart be troubled. *Col. 3:15,*
Proverb a4:23, 23:7.

Repent. Which means, change the way
you THINK! *Think the way God Thinks! Phil.2:5-*
Let the mind be in you, which was also in Christ
Jesus. Rom. 8:6- To be carnally minded is death;
but to be spiritually minded is life and peace.

Praise the Lord. *Is. 61:3, Ps. 34:3-5.*

Delight yourself in the Lord. *Ps. 37:4- ...he*
will give you the desires of your heart.

Commit your ways and Rest in the Lord.
Ps. 37:5, 37:7.

WAIT ON THE LORD. *Ps.* **37:1.**

The lord gives you strength to go through. *Ps. 41:10.*

What your weapon is NOT: *II Cor. 10:4 -5 - The weapons of our warfare are not carnal, but mighty through God to the pulling down of STRONG HOLDS.*

Who you are fighting against. *Eph. 6:12 - For we wrestle not against flesh and blood, but against principalities, again powers, against the rulers of the darkness of this world, against spiritual wickedness in high places. II Cor. 10:3.*

Do not walk weary. *Gal.6:9, Heb. 12:3.*

God can do above all that we can ASK OR THINK according to the power that he has given us. *Eph. 3:20*

Put on the whole armor of God. *Eph. 6:14 -15* **ALWAYS PRAY and NOT FAINT! Eph.** *5:18, PHIL. 4:6, I THES. 5:7.*

WATCH your thoughts. *Phil.4:8-9*

GIVE THANKS. I Thess. 5:18

If we can see it, it is temporary II Cor. 4:18

Do not to let the root of bitterness spring up. Heb. 12:15

Come boldly to the throne of GRACE in the time of need. Heb. 12:15

Jesus is the Healer. Is. 53: 4 -5

God is with us, carrying us THOUGH! IS. 43:2-3 WE ARE NOT ALONE!

Now that I have walked out that part of my journey, I am still have to remember all of these things in God's Word. For His Word keeps me. I have and continue blooming where I find myself planted; always trusting God for His rest and peace. Know This: Never! Never! Ever Give Up! When you are on the mountain journeys of life, choose to continue moving up to the top, instead of standing still or going back. God is taking us to the top for a reason. The top is your VICTORY! Standing Still - Makes you stagnated. Stagnation causes you to have an unpleasant odor and does not allow people to see Christ in you. No one wants you to be around people who smell. Going Back - Signals Failure! As children of God, we want to live a victorious life. Driving while looking behind you is not a very smart thing to do. That's why the front windshield in a car is bigger than the rear view mairrow. Keep your focus on what is ahead. The Lord knows His plans for our future. Jer. 29:11

HEALING SCRIPTURES THAT WORK

He said, "If you carefully listen to the voice of the Lord your God, and do what is right in His eyes, and if you pay close attention to His commands and keep all His decrees, I will not bring on you any of the diseases that I brought on the Egyptians, for I am the Lord Who heals you!" Exodus 15:26 Surely He took up our infirmities or sicknesses and carried out sorrows, yet we considered Him stricken by God, and smitten by Him and afflicted. But, He was pierced for our transgressions; He was crushed for our iniquities/sins; the punishment that brought us peace was upon Him, and by His wounds we are healed! Isaiah 53:4-5

Beloved, I pray that in all respects you may prosper and be in good health, just as your soul prospers. 3 John 2

The thief comes only to steal, kill, and destroy; <u>I came</u> that they might have life, and have it more abundantly! John 10:10

"<u>Have faith in God,</u>" Jesus answered. "I tell you the truth, if anyone says to this mountain, 'Go, throw yourself into the sea,' and does not doubt in His heart but believes that what he says will happen,<u> it will be done for him.</u> Therefore, I tell you, <u>whatever</u> you ask in prayer, believe that your receive it, and you will!" Mark 11:22-24

My son, pay attention to what I say; listen closely to my words. Do not let them out of your sight; keep them within your heart; <u>for they are life to those who find them, and health to a man's whole body.</u> Proverbs 4:20-22

So faith comes from hearing and hearing by the Word of God. Romans 10:17

Ask, and it will be given to you; seek, and you will find; knock, and the door will be opened to you. For if you being evil, know how to give good gifts to your children, how much more shall your Father in heaven, give good gifts to them that ask! Matthew 7:7-11

Jesus said to him, "I will go and heal him." Then Jesus said to the centurion, "Go! It will be done just as you believed it would." And his servant was healed at that very hour. This was to fulfill what was spoken through the prophet Isaiah: He took up our infirmities/sicknesses, and carried our diseases. Matthew 8:7, 13, 17

Then He touched their eyes and said, "According to your faith will it be done for you." Jesus went through all the towns and villages, teaching in their synagogues, preaching the good news of the kingdom, and healing every disease and sickness among the people. Matthew 9:29, 35

When Jesus landed and saw a large crowd, He had compassion on them and healed their sick. Matthew 14:14

Great crowds came to Him, bringing them lame, the blind, the crippled, the mute and many others, and laid them at His feet; <u>and He healed them.</u> Matthew 15:30

Then the disciples came to Jesus in private and asked, "Why couldn't we drive it out?" He replied, "Because you have so little faith. I tell you the truth, if you have faith as small as a mustard seed, you can say to this mountain, move from here to there, and it will move. <u>Nothing will be impossible for you."</u> Matthew 17:19-21

And great multitudes followed Him; and He healed them there. Matthew 19:2

Jesus went throughout Galilee, teaching in their synagogues, preaching the good news of the kingdom, and healing every disease and sickness among the people. News about Him spread all over Syria, and people brought to Him all who will ill with various diseases, those suffering severe pain, the demon possessed, those having seizures, and the paralyzed, and <u>He healed them.</u> Matthew 4:23-24

And Jesus healed many who were sick with various diseases. He drove out many demons, but He would not let the demons speak because they knew Who He was. Mark 1:34

And He said to her, "Daughter, your faith has healed you. Go in peace and be healed of your affliction." Mark 5:34

And Jesus said to him, "Go your way; <u>your faith has made you well."</u> And immediately he received his sight and began following Him along the road. Mark 10:52

"If you can?" said Jesus. <u>"Everything is possible for him who believes."</u> Mark 9:23

Power was coming from Him <u>and healing them all.</u> Luke 6:19

And I will do whatever you ask in My name, so that the Father may be glorified in the

Son. You may ask Me for anything in My name, and I will do it. John 14:13-14

You know how Jesus of Nazareth was anointed by God with power, and the Holy Spirit and how He went about doing good, and healing all who were oppressed by the devil, for God was with Him. Acts 10:38

Christ has redeemed us from the curse of the law by becoming a curse for us, for it is written, "Cursed is everyone who is hung on a tree." Galatians 3:13

Jesus is the same yesterday, today and forever! Hebrews 13:8

But for you who revere My Name, the Son of Righteousness will rise with healing in His wings, and you will go out and leap like calves released from the stalls! Malachi 4:2

Blessed is he whose transgressions are forgiven, whose sins are covered. Blessed is the man whose sin the Lord does not count against him, and in whose spirit there is no lie. When I kept silent about my sin, my bones wasted away, through my groaning all day long. For day and night Your hand was heavy upon me; my strength was drained away as in the heat of summer. Then I acknowledged my sin to You and did not cover up my iniquity. I said, "I will confess my transgressions to the Lord." And You forgave the guilt of my sin. Therefore, let everyone who is godly pray to You while you may be found; surely when the flood waters rise, they will not reach him. <u>You are my hiding place;</u> You will protect me from trouble, and surround me with songs of deliverance. (Selah) I will instruct you and teach you in the way you should go; I will counsel you with My eye upon you. Do not be like the horse or the mule, which have no understanding, but must be controlled by bit and bridle, or they will not come to you. Many are the sorrows of the wicked, <u>but the Lord's unfailing</u>

love surrounds the man who trusts in Him. Be glad in the Lord, and rejoice you righteous ones, and shout for joy, all you who are upright in heart! Psalm 32

If you make the Most High your dwelling—even the Lord, who is my refuge—then no evil will befall you, nor will any plague come near your tent. Psalm 91:9-10

Why are you in despair, O' my soul? Why so disturbed within me? Put your hope in God, for I will yet praise Him, my Savior and my God. Psalm 42:11

Have mercy on me, O' Lord, for I am weak. O' Lord heal me, for my bones are in agony. Psalm 6:2

As for me, I said, "O' Lord, have mercy on me; Heal my soul, for I have sinned against You." Psalm 41:4

Bless the Lord, O' my soul, and forget not all His benefits, who forgives all your sins, and heals all your diseases. Psalm 103:2-3

Do not be wise in your own eyes; fear the Lord, and turn away from evil. <u>This will bring healing to your body and strength to your bones.</u> Proverbs 3:7-8

And the prayer offered in faith will make the sick person well. The Lord will raise up. If he has sinned, he will be forgiven. James 5:15

For He Himself bore our sins on the cross, so that we might die to sins and live for righteousness; <u>For by His wounds we are healed!</u> I Peter 2:24

Heal me, O' Lord, and I shall be healed; Save me, and I shall be saved, for You are my praise. Jeremiah 17:14

Little children, you are of God, and have overcome them, for He who is in you, is greater than he who is in the world. I John 4:4

Then God said, "Let us make man in Our image, according to Our likeness; and let them rule over the fish of the sea, and over the birds of the sky, and over the cattle, and over all the earth, and over every creeping thing that creeps upon the earth. Genesis 1:26

You have given him dominion over the works of Your hands; You have put <u>all things</u> under his feet. Psalm 8:6

But we see Jesus, who was made a little lower than the angels, now crowned with glory and honor, because He suffered death so that by the grace of God, He might taste death for all men. Hebrews 2:9

Submit yourselves therefore to God. Resist the devil, and he will flee from you. James 4:7

My purpose is that they may be encouraged in heart and united in love, so that they may have the full riches of complete understanding in order that they may know the mystery of God, namely Christ Himself, in who are hidden all the treasures of wisdom and knowledge. So then just as you received Christ Jesus as Lord, continue to live in Him, rooted, and built up in Him, strengthened in the faith as you were taught, *and overflowing with gratitude and thankfulness!* See to it that no one takes you captive through hollow and deceptive philosophy, which depends on human tradition and the basic principles of this world rather than on Christ. For in Christ all the fullness of the Deity lives in bodily form and you are complete in Christ, Who is the head over every power and authority. When you were dead in your sins, and in your sin nature, God made you alive with Christ. He forgave us all our sins, having cancelled the written code, with its regulations, that was against us, and stood opposed to us; He took it away, nailing it to the cross. And having disarmed the powers and authorities, He made a public spectacle of them, triumphing over them through the cross. Therefore, do not let anyone judge you by what you eat or drink or with regard to a religious festival, a new moon celebration or a Sabbath Day. These are a shadow of the things that were to come; <u>the reality, however, is found in Christ!</u> Colossians 2:2-3, 6-10, 13-17

He sent forth His Word, and healed them; He rescued them from the grave. Psalm 107:20

And the Lord will remove from you all sickness; and He will not put on you any of the terrible diseases of Egypt. Deuteronomy 7:15

A merry heart does good like a medicine, but a crushed and broken spirit dries up the bones. Proverbs 17:22

Go back and tell Hezekiah, the leader of My people, "This is what the Lord, the God of your Father David says, "I have heard your prayers, and seen your tears; <u>I will heal you!</u>" On the third day from now you will go up to the house of the Lord. 2 Kings 20:5